MADE OF MAGIC

Written by Anjana Vasan

Illustrated by Kelsey Marshalsey

Hardcover ISBN: 978-1-7386606-0-5

Digital ISBN: 978-1-7386606-1-2

Paperback ISBN: 978-1-7386606-2-9

To every rainbow baby out there,
you're a dream come true.

Today, I'm going to tell you a secret
About how you were made.
Listen closely,
You'll be amazed.

I wanted you forever,
To love, kiss, and snuggle.
But I didn't know how to make you,
It was quite a struggle.

So, I made a wish,
To a good-hearted witch.

She said,
"Gather all these things, you'll get your kid."
And that's what I did.

plant bluebells
sunshine
elephants gift
dolphins kiss
look to the stars
unicorns magic
your love

First, I went to the garden,
And planted some bluebells.
So, you'll remember to care,
About the planet, people, and even the bears.

I want you to be happy.
So, I got sunshine from the sky

To help you find joy,
Even when you cry.

Next on the list
Was an elephant's gift.

He said, "If your friends want to play,

Don't forget to share."
After all, that's only fair.

Then the elephant pushed me,
With his large, long trunk.

So, I pressed onward
With all my spunk!

For some fun, I couldn't miss
Swimming in the ocean for a dolphin's kiss!

So, you can find ways to laugh and play,
Especially on days that may be a little grey.

You should be free
To be who you are.
So, I looked to the stars
To help you fly.
They said...

Finally, I needed two more things,
To make you YOU!
A unicorn's magic,

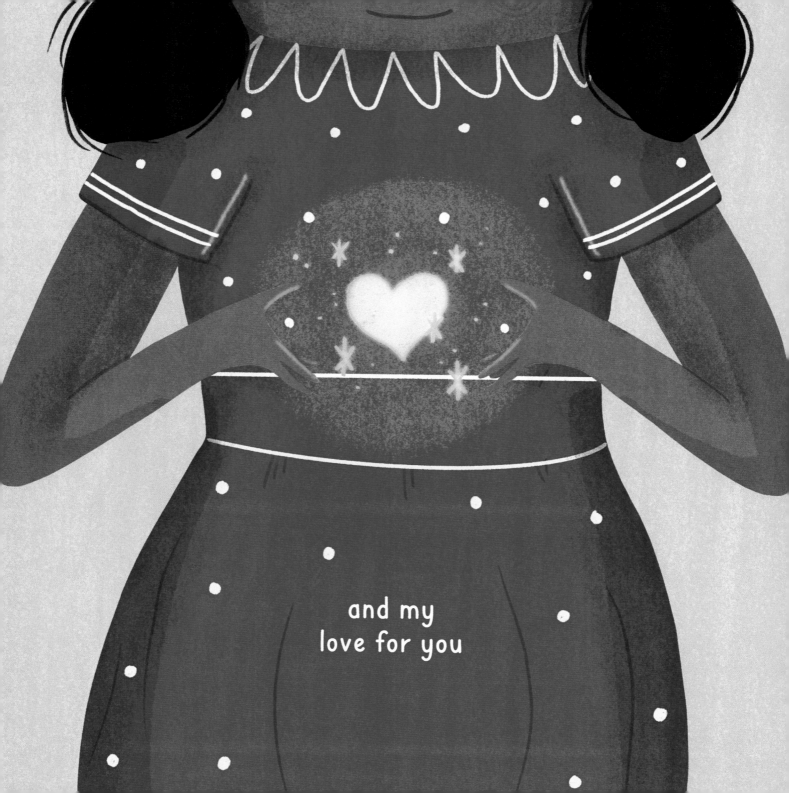

So, I walked on a rainbow,
Hoping you will grow.
And counted

one,

two,

three

With just a little help from the good-hearted witch,
I waited until

You fell from the skies!

Made in the USA
Las Vegas, NV
09 March 2023

68776576R00017